Stress

Peace amid Pressure

RCL Ministry Booklets

Booklets by Jeffrey S. Black, Michael R. Emlet, Walter Henegar, Robert D. Jones, Susan Lutz, James C. Petty, David Powlison, Darby A. Strickland, Paul David Tripp, Edward T. Welch, and John Yenchko.

ADD
Anger
Angry at God?
Bad Memories
Depression
Domestic Abuse
Forgiveness
God's Love
Guidance
Homosexuality
"Just One More"
Marriage
Motives
OCD
Pornography
Pre-Engagement
Priorities
Procrastination
Prodigal Children
Self-Injury
Sexual Sin
Stress
Suffering
Suicide
Teens and Sex
Thankfulness
Why Me?
Why Worry?
Worry

See all the books and booklets in the Resources for Changing Lives series at www.prpbooks.com

Stress

Peace amid Pressure

David Powlison

RCL Ministry Booklets
Susan Lutz, Series Editor

P&R PUBLISHING
P.O. BOX 817 • PHILLIPSBURG • NEW JERSEY 08865-0817

© 2004 by David Powlison

All rights reserved. No part of this booklet may be reproduced, stored in a retrieval system, or transmitted in any form or by any means—electronic, mechanical, photocopy, recording, or otherwise—except for brief quotations for the purpose of review or comment, without the prior permission of the publisher, P&R Publishing Company, P.O. Box 817, Phillipsburg, New Jersey 08865-0817.

Scripture quotations are from the *NEW AMERICAN STANDARD BIBLE®*. ©Copyright The Lockman Foundation 1960, 1962, 1963, 1968, 1971, 1972, 1973, 1975, 1977, 1995. Used by permission.

Printed in the United States of America

Library of Congress Cataloging-in-Publication Data

Powlison, David, 1949–
Stress : peace amid pressure / David Powlison.
p.   cm. — (Resources for changing lives)
Includes bibliographical references.
ISBN-10: 0-87552-660-8 (pbk.)
ISBN-13: 978-0-87552-660-7
1. Bible. O.T. Psalms CXXXI—Criticism, interpretation, etc. I. Title. II. Series.

BS1430.52.P68 2004
223'.206—dc22
2004048368

LORD,
my heart is not proud,
and my eyes are not haughty,
and I do not go after things too great
and too difficult for me.
Surely I have composed and quieted my soul,
like a weaned child on his mother,
like a weaned child on me is my soul.
Israel, hope in the LORD now and forever.
Psalm 131 (author's translation)

God speaks to us in many different ways. When you hear, "Now it came to pass," settle down for a good story. When God asserts, "I Am," trust his self-revelation. When he promises, "I will," bank on it. When he tells you, "You shall . . . you shall not," do what he says.

Psalm 131 is in a different vein. In it, God gives us intimate access to the inner life of someone who has learned composure. This person is quiet on the inside because he has learned the only true and lasting peace. He describes what the peace that passes understanding is like (Phil. 4:7), and invites us to enter in.

Amazingly, this man isn't noisy inside. He isn't busy, busy, busy. Not obsessed or on edge. Pressures to achieve don't consume him. Failure and despair don't haunt him. Anxiety isn't spinning him into free fall. Regrets don't corrode his inner experience. He's not stumbling through the minefield of blind longings and fears.

He's quiet.

Are you quiet inside? Is Psalm 131 your experience, too? If your answer is No, what is the "noise" going on inside you? Where does it come from? How do you get busy and preoccupied? Why do you lose your composure? When do you get worried, irritable, wearied, or hopeless? How can you regain composure?

We'll get to these questions, because they are what Psalm 131 answers. The psalm is show-and-tell for how to become peaceful inside. But let's dip our toes in the water before taking the plunge.

About the Psalm

First, think about who is talking to us in Psalm 131. We are listening to the inner conversation of someone whom God called "a man after his own heart" (1 Sam. 13:14). In other words, this man processes life the way we're meant to. That makes him worth listening to.

David wrote the original words 3000 years ago. The psalm bears the heading, *A Song of Ascents, of David*. Like others of David's most memorable psalms—16, 23, 31, 32, 103, 139—Psalm 131 captures the quintessence of one piece of human experience. We know many things about David, but two characteristics stand out. First, the Lord chose David, anointed him, loved him, and blessed him. God was *with* David. Second, David knew this Lord. He referred his life to God; he walked *with* God. Such a man lets you into his stream of consciousness.

A millennium later, someone else lived this psalm even more fully. Update the heading: *A Song of Ascents, of Jesus*. Psalm 131 expresses Jesus' life experience, the inner workings of his consciousness. Think about that. The Father's chosen, anointed, loved, and blessed Son lets you listen in. In Psalm 131, God who became a man thinks out loud for you. This isn't just an exhortation about how to think with the mind of Christ. Jesus' own internal peacemaking happens in front of your eyes.

Second, get a clear picture of what Psalm 131 is *not*. It does not portray unruffled detachment or stoic indifference. It's not about having an easygoing personality or low expectations. It's not retreat from the troubles of life or retirement to a life of ease. It's not the quieting of inner noise that a glass of wine or a daily dose of Prozac produces. After all, Jesus and David were both kingdom-builders who expected—and achieved—huge things in the midst of commotion and trouble. They experienced pressure, joy, heartache, outrage, affection, and courage. So Psalm 131's inner quiet comes in the midst of actions, relationships, and problems.

Third, understand rightly what Psalm 131 describes. *This composure is learned, and it is learned in relationship.* Such purposeful quiet is achieved, not spontaneous. It is conscious, alert, and chosen. It is a form of self-mastery by the grace of God: "Surely I have composed and quieted my soul." And it happens in living relationship with Someone Else. You are "discipled" into such composure. Listen and watch carefully. You'll come to understand a form of self-mastery that arises only in relationship. Can *you* get to this quieted place, here and now, in your actual life? Yes. This psalm is from a man who leads you by the hand. The last sentence of the psalm stops talking with God and talks to you. Psalm 131 aims to become your words as a chosen and blessed child. We'll look closely at the dynamic. Psalm 131 contains big things in a very tiny package, divided into three parts.

Deliverance from Noise

LORD,
> *my heart is not proud,*
> *and my eyes are not haughty,*
> *and I do not go after things too great*
> > *and too difficult for me.*
> > *Psalm 131:1*

Faith delivers you from your biggest problem, a proud self-will. David says to the Lord, "I am *not* self-trusting, opinionated, and headstrong. I am *not* superior to others. I am *not* attempting the impossible." The process through which he was tamed is still implicit (until vs. 2). The reason for such astonishing composure and humility is still implicit (until vs. 3). We see the results first, and are intrigued. David is quiet. He has consciously distanced himself from everything that rattles inside us. To be able to say, "I am *not* something," you must learn to identify the thing you are not.

A pool of water in the stillness of dawn is highly sensitive to vibration. Watch the surface and you can detect the approach of the slightest breeze or a slight tremor in the ground. You locate the wriggling of a fish you cannot see or a tiny water bug skating over the surface. In the same way, this quiet psalm can make you highly sensitive to "noise." It is an instrument with which to detect gusts, tremors, or thrashing in the soul. What makes us so noisy inside? Turn the psalm into its opposite, the anti-psalm:

> Self,
>> my heart is proud (I'm absorbed in myself),
>> and my eyes are haughty (I look down on other people),
>> and I chase after things too great and too difficult for me.
>> So of course I'm noisy and restless inside; it comes naturally,

> like a hungry infant fussing on his
> mother's lap,
> like a hungry infant, I'm restless
> with my demands and worries.
> I scatter my hopes onto anything
> and everybody all the time.

Noisiness makes perfect sense. You can identify exactly where the rattling noises come from.

Do you remember *Alice in Wonderland*, how Alice was either too big or too small? Because she was never quite the right size, she was continually disoriented. We all have that problem. We are the wrong size. We imagine ourselves to be independent and autonomous: *proud hearts*. We become engrossed in monstrous trivialities of our own devising. We pursue grandiosities and glories. One of the symptoms of the disease is that we become noisy inside.[1] Seventeenth-century English had a great word for stirring up much ado about nothing: *vainglory*. Or, in Macbeth's bitter words: "Life's but a walking shadow, a poor player, that struts and frets his hour upon the stage, and then is heard no more; it is a tale told by an idiot, full of sound and fury, signifying nothing" (V:5).

Of course, this doesn't seem like much of a problem while we busily telemarket our pride to ourselves and others. "I just want a little respect and appreciation. Of course I want the home appliances to work and the car mechanic to be honest. That's pretty normal. I want approval and understanding. Is that too much to ask? I want the church to thrive and my sermon to go well. It's for God, after all. I want satisfaction and compensation for the ways others did me wrong. I don't want much. If only I had better health, a little more money, a more meaningful job, nicer clothes, and a restful vacation, then I'd be satisfied. I want a measure of success—just a bit of recognition—as an athlete, a beauty, an intellectual, a musician, a leader, a mother. I want control. Who doesn't? I want to feel good. Doesn't God want me to feel good? I want to have more self-confidence, to believe in myself. I want . . . well, I want MY WAY. I WANT THE GOODIES. I WANT GLORY. I WANT GOD TO DO MY WILL. I WANT TO BE GOD . . . Doesn't everybody?"

Our slavery to the corruption that is in the world by lust (2 Peter 1:4) seems so plausible. Our restless disorientation seems so natural, so desirable. But it's noisy. The noise tips us off to what's going on. The static of anxiety, irritation, despondency, or ambition makes sense from within the logic of a proud heart. If you are *not* proud, then quietness and composure make sense.

It also goes with the territory that we are opinionated, routinely judging and belittling others: *haughty eyes*. Pride is not just about ME. It's also about you. I must look down on you in some way. Our absorption in judgmental opinions runs very deep. Pride says, "I'm right in myself." Haughty eyes say, "I'm right compared to you." Have you noticed that even people who feel lousy about themselves are judgmental toward others? When you feel inferior to others, you don't respect them or treat them with mercy. Instead, you envy, hate, grumble, and criticize. Even self-belittling tendencies— "low self-esteem," self-pity, self-hatred, timidity, fears of failure and rejection—fundamentally express *pride* failing, *pride* intimidated, and *pride* despairing. Such pride, even when much battered, still finds someone else to look down on.

A friend of mine once vividly described this problem. She said that she had almost no true peers, people with whom she related eye-to-eye. Her relationships were not characterized by generosity, candor, or trust. There were a few "pedestal people" in her life, people she thought could do no wrong. There were many,

many "pit people" in her life, people she looked down on for one reason or another. The two categories were connected only by an elevator shaft! A person could fall off the pedestal and end up in the pit. She had a long history of disappointment in every relationship. Unsurprisingly, she was a woman with a lot of inner noise: fretful, self-absorbed, easily offended, depressed, competitive. But as she grew in Christ, she grew in composure. As she learned to live in the way of peace, lo and behold, she began to discover peers and to build friendships.

Another way of putting this is to say that she stopped *pursuing impossibilities*. That's the third phrase in Psalm 131:1: not going after things that are beyond you, "things too great and too wonderful" (author's translation). Even the small, everyday things that everyone races after are, in fact, "beyond us." From your daily bread to your abilities and opportunities, these are gifts from God that you don't control. What happens when you attempt to control another person's attitudes and choices? You set yourself up for despair or rage, anxiety or short-lived euphoria, suspicion or manipulation. What happens when you attempt to ensure that you will not get sick and die? You become obsessed with diet and exercise, or litigious toward doctors, or plagued with fear that any nagging pain might be the one that finally gets you. What happens when you are obsessed with getting people to like you? You become flirtatious or artificial, a coward or a deceiver, a chameleon or a recluse. What happens when you live for success in sports, career, or your physical appearance? You get injured. You retire. Someone comes along who is better than you. You get old and wrinkled. You die.

How different things are when you pursue what you are called to pursue! You've discovered what you're made for. You have composure. Paul put it this way, "Flee from youthful lusts and pursue righteousness, faith, love and peace, with those who call on the Lord from a pure heart" (2 Tim. 2:22). When you go after the right things, you'll find what you're looking for.

The Process of Peace

Surely I have composed and quieted my
soul,
 like a weaned child on his mother,
 like a weaned child on me is my soul.
 Psalm 131:2

Having seen the result, we now see the process. Quiet your noisy self to know the peace that passes understanding. To gain composure is to go through a weaning process. Something that once meant everything comes to mean nothing. What is this composing, this quieting, this weaning?

Notice that you are definitively different at the end of the process. You aren't "sort of composed, sort of quiet, sort of weaned." You once were noisy, and now you've learned quiet. We always learn through a process, but in principle there are not gradations. You either know how to quiet yourself or you stay noisy. You're either a nursing infant or a weaned child. In the first word in Psalm 131:2, translated as *Surely*, David comes close to taking an oath: "If I don't . . . If this isn't so, then . . . I swear that . . . !" David means it. He is bound and determined to wrestle down his unruly soul.

Dying to your restless, fretful, and irritable ways does not come easily. There is no automatic formula or pat answer. To *compose* your soul means literally to level it. Bulldoze the building site. Get a grip. When Jesus said, "Peace, be still" to the stormy lake, he smoothed the turbulence. To *quiet* your soul means to silence the noise and tumult.

"Sssshhh" to your desires, fears, opinions, anxieties, agendas, and irritabilities. We looked in detail at the assertions David made about himself in the first verse. Now we see that David had gone about unplugging the noise machines and knocking down the ladders. This sort of composure and quietness is not apathy, but alertness. It is conscious, not unconscious. It is self-mastery by grace, not sleepy ease.

How do you purify your heart? How does a proud heart become humble? Not by doing penance. Not by beating on yourself or resolving to mend your ways. You can do all those things and still be proud. You cannot destroy the tumult of self-will by sheer will: "I will stop being irritable. I will stop being fretful. I will stop imposing my will on the universe." Can the leopard change its spots? You are not strong enough; you are too strong. The only way you can wrestle yourself down is by the promises of God. You need help the way a drowning man needs help from outside himself to rescue him.

Only one thing is strong enough to overpower a stormy life: what God promises to do in and through Jesus Christ. It is by great and precious promises that we escape the corruption that is in the world by lust (2 Peter 1:4). From God's side, we escape ourselves by being loved by Jesus Christ through the powerful presence of the Holy Spirit. From our side, we escape ourselves by learning a lifestyle of intelligent repentance, genuine faith, and specific obedience.

In the 1700s, Katarina von Schlegel wrote a hymn about wrestling to compose and quiet her soul. It is an extended personalization of Psalm 131:2, presumably written in the context of some great loss.

> Be still, my soul: the Lord is on thy side;
> bear patiently the cross of grief or pain;
> leave to thy God to order and provide;
> in every change, he faithful will remain.
> Be still, my soul: thy best, thy heavenly Friend
> through thorny ways leads to a joyful end.

Think about that, and still yourself. Remember the Lord's favor, control, fidelity, and friendship. Remain patient in your sufferings.

> Be still, my soul: thy God doth undertake
> to guide the future as he has the past.
> Thy hope, thy confidence let nothing shake;
> all now mysterious shall be bright at last.
> Be still, my soul: the waves and winds still know
> his voice who ruled them while he dwelt below.

Why does she have to keep reminding herself, "Be still, my soul"? We need to be stilled. Who is strong enough to rule the things that wail, rattle, or shout within us? Only God, who is purposively active in his children. He will have the final say. Christ ruled the storms, rules them still, and will rule them. You can trust Someone Else amid your present uncertainties.

> Be still, my soul: when dearest friends depart,
> and all is darkened in the vale of tears,
> then shalt thou better know his love, his heart,
> who comes to soothe thy sorrow and thy fears.

> Be still, my soul: thy Jesus can repay
> from his own fullness all he takes
> > away.

Perhaps irreparable loss is the hardest thing to face. A loved one dies, and will never again walk through the door to greet you. You retire, and can never again return to the work into which you poured your talent, time, and concern. You will never again be young. No second chance to do your college years or that failed marriage over again. Such things devastate us. Can you quiet yourself? Jesus gives you himself.

> Be still, my soul: the hour is hast'ning
> > on
> when we shall be forever with the
> > Lord,
> when disappointment, grief, and fear
> > are gone,
> sorrow forgot, love's purest joys re-
> > stored.
> Be still, my soul: when change and
> > tears are past,
> all safe and blessed we shall meet at last.

Katarina von Schlegel was the ultimate realist. Most of the noise in our souls is generated by our attempts to control the uncontrollable. We grasp after the wind. We rage, fear, and finally despair. But this wise sister focused on an enduring hope. Be still, my soul. All that is hard now will be forgotten amid love's purest joys. This slight, momentary affliction is preparing for us an eternal weight of glory beyond all comparison (2 Cor. 4:17). Psalm 131 faith lives with eyes open.

David drives this home with a wonderful metaphor: *like a weaned child on his mother, like a weaned child, my soul rests on me.* The original sentence emphasizes the parallelism and does not even contain the verb "rests": "Like a weaned child on his mother, like a weaned child on me my soul." Most of us have seen a nursing child before the weaning process begins. For those of you who are mothers, this image is particularly evocative. When a hungry child is placed on his mother's lap, he is agitated. He roots around, squirming anxiously. If he doesn't get immediate satisfaction, he frets and fusses. Mother's milk means life, health, satisfaction, joy. If mother doesn't deliver right now, he'll thrash about. His emotions range over the whole spectrum of noisy, negative emotion, the childish versions of things that destroy adults: anxiety, depression, anger, jealousy, discontent, and confusion. We've all seen that.

But have you ever seen that same child when he is successfully weaned? A dramatic change has taken place. Now the child rests upon his mother, quiet and at peace (assuming she's spooning in the solid food!). The child has *changed*. Envision your own soul as a small child sitting on your lap. You used to be noisy, squirmy, and demanding. Now you sit still. That's the picture of learning peace.

The Reason for Peace

Israel, hope in the LORD *now and forever. Psalm 131:3*

We looked first at the result, and then at the process. This last line gives the reason. The Lord, Jesus Christ, is your hope. Pride dies as the humility of faith lives. Haughtiness lowers its eyes as the dependency of hope lifts up its eyes. You stop pursuing impossibilities when you start pursuing certainties. This simple sentence distills wonders. Consider the command and invitation you are now receiving.

First, you are called by name. *Israel* originally named an insignificant family of nomads.

Later it identified a mildly significant buffer state in the ancient Near East. But now the scope of Psalm 131:3 extends to every nation, tribe, tongue, and people. That includes you. We are all called to set our hope in the Lord now and forever. Sometimes Jesus applies the old name to his new people: "the Israel of God" (Gal. 6:16), or the Jew inwardly, with a circumcised heart (Rom. 2:29). But now we are more commonly called by other names:

- Beloved
- Chosen
- Holy ones (set apart to the Holy One; "saints")
- Sons and daughters
- Brothers and sisters
- Slaves
- Called out ones ("church")
- Disciples

Disciple is the name most commonly used to describe you. You intentionally learn and change as you live with your teacher-for-life, Jesus Christ.[2]

Second, you are called to *hope in the Lord*. Who is this person who topples all the ladders to nowhere and gives you something better?

He is the true God, the only Redeemer from the idols we construct. Your hope is in "I AM," who becomes known simply as "the Lord." Eventually, he more immediately and personally names himself: Jesus Christ is Lord.

What exactly are you to hope for? Psalm 131 is very condensed, stating the general principle without any specifics beyond the Person. You are free to particularize the content of hope with promises from throughout the Bible. But it would probably be wisest to start in the immediate vicinity. Psalm 131 is intentionally paired with Psalm 130, which gives details about what exactly we are to hope in (in italics).

> Out of the depths I have cried to *You,*
>   *O L*ORD.
> Lord, *hear my voice!*
> Let *Your ears be attentive*
> To the voice of my supplications.
> If You, LORD, should mark iniquities,
> O LORD, who could stand?
> But *there is forgiveness with You,*
> That You may be feared.
> I wait *for the L*ORD, my soul does wait,
> And *in His word* do I hope.
> My soul waits *for the Lord*

> More than the watchmen for the
> morning;
> Indeed, more than the watchmen for
> the morning.
> O Israel, hope *in the* L<small>ORD</small>,
> For *with the* L<small>ORD</small> *there is lovingkindness*,
> And *with Him is abundant redemption.*
> And *He will redeem Israel*
> From *all his iniquities.*

The things in italics invite your hope. You will not go wrong if you fulfill Psalm 131:3 by living out Psalm 130. The sense of need, the eager anticipation, and the inner tension of waiting effectively illustrate what Psalm 131's composure is like. We are racehorses, not milk cows, called to equine alertness and focus, not bovine placidity and apathy!

Third, you are called to such hopes *now and forever*. David speaks in a generality, literally, "from now until forever." That pretty much covers the territory! But the time frame of our hope is even more clearly defined than David could have known. We hope fully on the grace to be given at the revelation of Jesus Christ (1 Peter 1:13). Both *now* and *forever* shine with newer, brighter meanings for us who read Psalm 131 in the light of Christ.

Transpose this last line to include Christ as you personalize the psalm, for in him we have more details to inform intelligent faith.

Personalizing Psalm 131

Your biggest problem is proud self-will. That's the noise machine inside you. And there is a way to gain composure through the Lord. What should you do now so you can honestly say, "My heart is not proud"? How can you make this psalm your own? How do you quiet yourself?

First, identify the ladders to nowhere that pride erects.

- Where do you raise up ladders of *achievement*? How do you go for victory, for grades, for promotion, for the big church, for the idealized devotional life?
- Where do you clamber up ladders of *acquisition*? Where do you say "if only"? Where do you seek the goodies, the security, the recognition?
- Where do you race up ladders of *appetite*? Where do you gratify your need for ease or control? Where do you gratify hunger or lust or superiority?

- Where do you scuttle up ladders of *avoidance?* Where do you get away from poverty, rejection, suffering, and people?

Pride sets up these ladders and climbs on high. The inner static reveals where your pride is located. You feel nervously happy when you climb up a few rungs. You feel bitter and despairing when you land in a heap at the bottom. Haughty eyes look down on anyone below you on the ladders you most cherish. You freely criticize others about some things, but not everything. Those particular ladders from which you gaze down in disdain are *your* precious and proud aspirations. You feel envy or despair when anyone else rises (or threatens to rise) above you in some things, but not everything. You chase after impossibilities, matters too great and too wonderful. No wonder you are noisy inside. Stairs of sand look so good. They promise to take you someplace, but they collapse beneath the weight of your life.[3]

Second, come to know Jesus. He never climbed the ladders to nowhere. He's the iconoclast, the ladder-toppler, the idol-breaker, the lie-piercer, the pride-smasher. He gives life, makes peace, gives joy, and makes you over. Seek Jesus, carrying your sins in your hands.

Psalm 131 is his consciousness: quieted but not placid, composed but not detached. His composure is a communicable attribute, something he willingly teaches and gives away. Psalm 131 embodies a radical dynamic. It goes against everything we innately cherish, yet it gives us something worth cherishing forever. You need Jesus to liberate your heart in a coup-d'état. Psalm 131 overthrows the powers-that-be to establish the reign of Him-who-is.

This is a quiet little psalm, but it contains a revolutionary dynamic. Marx, Nietzsche, and Freud have been well described as "masters of suspicion." They rip veils off civilized, self-righteous complacency. They rattle the cage with counter-cultural analyses of the human condition. *Calvin and Hobbes*, *The Far Side*, and *Non Sequitur* give suspicion a touch of whimsy. Beats, hippies, existentialists, punks, and Goths try giving suspicion a viable lifestyle. They see something of what's wrong, and aim for something truer. But how can you criticize pride in others without being immolated in your own? When it comes to suspicion, only one person really pulls it off.

Jesus is the Master of masters of suspicion. And he's master of the lifestyle alternative, too. The Psalm 131 person engages in self-suspicion and social suspicion, toppling vainglory at every turn. But such a person ends in mirth and frolic, not cynicism and hypocrisy. Jesus gives you his own joy. His counterculture refreshes itself over the long haul. It has a principle of self-renewal: the demolition of pride, the creation of peace, humility, composure. "This is eternal life, that they may know you, the only true God, and Jesus Christ whom you have sent" (John 17:3). Jesus unveils our inner worlds and floods our hearts with light. He exposes both the self-righteously complacent and the self-righteously suspicious. He turns all the inner worlds upside down. He disassembles the noise machines. He saves you from yourself. He teaches you quiet. He gives you himself.

Third, live the mindset of Psalm 131. When you set your hope in the right place, you become the right size. No pride, no looking down from on high, no hot pursuit of pipe dreams. The soul-storms meet their Master: " 'Be quiet. Be still.' What is this? He commands even the demons, and they obey him! Who is this, that wind and sea obey him?" (see Mark 1:25–27, 4:39–41).

Psalms are meant to be read and quoted verbatim. Read Psalm 131 again. Read it slowly and take in each sentence.

LORD,
> *my heart is not proud,*
> *and my eyes are not haughty,*
> *and I do not go after things too great*
> > *and too difficult for me.*
> *Surely I have composed and quieted my*
> > *soul,*
> *like a weaned child on his mother,*
> *like a weaned child on me is my soul.*
> *Israel, hope in the LORD now and*
> > *forever.*

Memorize these words. It will take you only a few minutes to make them your own. Then turn these words over in your mind before drifting to sleep. Before counseling someone else. As you drive in your car. When you approach God to talk. When you get noisy inside for whatever reason. Read these words together in public worship. Preach or teach this psalm. Get the music, and sing this psalm with your brothers and sisters.

Psalms learned verbatim teach you to play "classical music," compositions practiced from the score, memorized, and played note-perfect. Psalms also intend to teach you how to play "jazz." Psalm 131 is a model as you improvise within your life experience. Most of life you make up as you go along. You'll probably say thousands of words out loud today. And that's nothing compared to the audio and video streaming continuously within your soul. Most of daily life is extemporaneous speech, not read from a manuscript. Few scenes in life are scripted, rehearsed, and recited. Psalm 131 is for jazz as well as classical. It gives a "for instance" for the rest of your thinking, sketching the general contours of a God-related life of dependent faith. You color in the living details, playing out personal variations on the Bible's theme. Create such inner conversations moment by moment. "Rejoice always, pray without ceasing, give thanks in all circumstances, because this is God's will for you in Christ Jesus" (1 Thess. 5:16–18). The Holy Spirit forms in you a psalm-generating heart and lifestyle. As you live in Christ in all circumstances, Jesus teaches you to think the way he does.

David Powlison *is the editor of* The Journal of Biblical Counseling *and a member of the faculty and counseling staff at the Christian Counseling & Educational Foundation in Glenside, Pennsylvania.*

Notes

1 Isaiah wrote, "The wicked are like the tossing sea, for it cannot be quiet, and its waters toss up refuse and mud. 'There is no peace,' says my God, 'for the wicked' " (57:20–21).
2 Interestingly, the name we most often use, "Christian," is used only three times in the Bible. It is a more impersonal name someone else might use to label you (Acts 11:26; Acts 26:28; 1 Peter 4:16). But these other names are intended to resonate more with your internal sense of identity-in-relationship.
3 In a wondrous image, Shakespeare's Bassanio speaks of all the deceptive show that arises because "hearts are all as false as stairs of sand." (*The Merchant of Venice*, III:2)

Resources for Changing Lives

A Ministry of
THE CHRISTIAN COUNSELING AND
EDUCATIONAL FOUNDATION
Glenside, Pennsylvania